The Ocean World of Jacques Cousteau

The Sea in Danger

man waste directly in the sea. In the United States alone, there are 9.2 million pleasure boats, 65,000 unregistered commercial fishing vessels, 46,000 registered commercial ships, and 1600 government-owned boats. The raw sewage from these craft is equal to that of a city with a population of about 650,000—the size of Boston.

In response to this problem, the Environmental Protection Agency proposed a standard for marine sanitary devices which requires that discharged effluent must produce a biological oxygen demand within certain limits and must have only a specified amount of suspended solids and a limited number of coliform bacteria. Such standards are less than ideal, but the hope is that once the notion of regulations is accepted, they can become stringent enough to be meaningful.

The EPA has also been active on another front in its effort to clean up the water. The agency has patented a process for purifying water that can be used by paper mills and other private polluters and which hopefully can be adapted for use by inland municipal sewage treatment plants. Called FACET, an acronym for fine activated carbon effluent treatment, the process was developed in a kraft paper mill but could have immediate applications in food-processing plants, petroleum operations, and organic chemical installations, all of which use water as a medium to carry and discharge wastes.

In the FACET process, the discharged water, instead of being channeled directly into a stream, is circulated through a series of tanks containing a slurry of finely ground activated carbon. The carbon, which can readily remove organic material from the water, is made by charring wood or coal. After the effluent is circulated through these tanks, the water is pure enough to be used again, which means that the system is self-contained and does not constantly draw on a river or lake for new water supplies.

The Environmental Protection Agency hopes eventually that the process could become compact enough so that it could be used in individual homes as a primary treatment stage before household wastes enter the municipal sewage system.

*Man's technology has produced **polluted water** with foamy heads, and now man's technology must be put to use to make that same water drinking pure.*

Rationalizing Land Use

Real estate booms can have very strange effects on regions, as we have become increasingly aware in recent years. But city planning, which has been a discipline largely ignored by builders, may yet have its day. A landscape architect, Ian McHarg, has come up with what appears to be a concrete and realistic approach to city planning and housing. The premise is that each place on earth is the sum of its historical, geological, and biological processes. These three factors must be taken into consideration if we are to make the best possible use of our land so that it is to both our advantage and nature's as well.

McHarg's solution is to map an area with an acetate overlay evaluating each criterion on a scale from one to three. Such factors as scenic beauty, geological stability, water table value, historical significance, biological productivity, and vital habitats are reflected in color density on the overlays. When all of the annotated overlays are stacked over the area map, a precise reading of a locality can be made. From this can be judged what the best use would be for all sections—what should be held out for wildlife refuges and parks, what is best for housing, schools, shopping centers, and highways.

The system was put to use in a land tract development outside Baltimore. There in 1962 a group of landowners who feared the spread of megalopolis to their 70-square-mile area formed the Green Spring and Worthington Valley Planning Council. An early study promised that with uncontrolled development the area would yield $33.5 million over a 20-year span. A plan based on the McHarg evaluations increased the potential yield by $7 million at the same time that it maintained the integrity of the area.

*Land in its **natural state** (above) can be left alone or wasted (below). Unproductive land, covered with lava, can be made into a useful **vineyard** (right).*

Clearing the Air

Black soot falling on homes, children choking as they play in a backyard, tearing eyes viewing the confluence of the Monongahela and Allegheny rivers as they form the mighty Ohio—all were part of an everyday scene in wartime Pittsburgh. Something, everyone agreed, had to be done about the steel mills and related industries that were polluting—even poisoning—the air. The decision was made as World War II was ending. The task took more than two decades to accomplish, but it was unquestionably a success. A combination of civic-minded citizens, tough-minded legislators, concerned businessmen, and cooperative industrial plants proved that something could be done about a city with badly polluted air.

Waste products were turned into profitable or reusable by-products. Catalytic converters, electric grids, and particle traps helped remove offensive matter from the air. Refined and revised techniques reduced the sources of pollution. It was costly, and it took a singularly concerted effort. There are cities, like Gary, Indiana, which are plagued by the same problems that troubled Pittsburgh, but remain polluted because the various interests can't get together. The city is smaller and poorer than Pittsburgh; the offending steel mills are only branch operations and not headquarters as they were in Pittsburgh. And, because of Gary's size, the blue-collar workers are afraid to rebel because they might lose their jobs, and the city might lose a taxpaying corporation.

*The emissions from some industrial smokestacks are strong enough and sufficiently corrosive to **peel paint** (opposite) from houses and automobiles.*

*A **geyser** (right) is not only not an air polluter, but it may be a source of electrical energy, for geothermal electrical plants are already in operation.*

Steel mills are not the only polluters. Electrical utilities are equally high on the list, primarily because of their consumption of low-cost, high-sulfur fuel. Because of this, there has been considerable interest in obtaining electrical power by harnessing geothermal energy. Tapping the earth's heat is not without its problems, but a U.S. government report said the process appears to be potentially less adverse to the environment than using conventional coal, oil, and nuclear means of producing electricity. Using geothermal energy to produce steam, which turns the turbines that generate electrical power, has already been accomplished in many areas of the world, but only on a small scale. One of the problems in using the earth's heat is that it might interfere with the balance of the rocks beneath the surface, which is especially true if the source of the energy is super-heated underground water like geysers. Thus, while air pollution from fossil fuel plants and thermal pollution from nuclear plants could theoretically be eliminated, there is a problem of disrupting the internal working of the earth since no one can predict what the long-range effects would be. The use of geothermal energy, then, is at best a stopgap measure until better and more economical methods of utilizing solar energy are developed.

Cars That Don't Kill

Pollution-free automobiles and other vehicles or aircraft have been a dream of inventors ever since the emissions of internal combustion engines have come to light. There have been many proposals to alleviate the situation, such as electric cars, steam cars, and engines running on propane. More than one ingenious driver has converted his automobile from burning gasoline to burning wastes for power, but none of these ideas has been picked up by the large auto manufacturers. One of the more serious suggestions is that of the rotary engine, which is not really any cleaner than the standard piston-driven internal combustion motor,

*Cars with **internal combustion engines** are less than a century old, yet they have made their mark in many ways (below). Now we are trying to clean up some of the more pernicious effects (above).*

but its compact size allows the installation of additional equipment such as catalytic converters and afterburners, which can reduce the amount of emissions. Most cars are still burning gasoline, but special additives like lead-tetraethyl have been eliminated in order to reduce the amount of some of the more harmful emissions.

The only way to really reduce the amount of such exhaust pollutants, however, is to reduce the number of internal combustion engines that are operating each day. As large-sized cities have found the dangers of smog and of increased carbon monoxide levels, the answer has become more apparent: mass transportation. The notion that each person has to drive to and from work each day is a

throwback to the time when every man had his own horse—which emitted a certain type of pollution, too, only that pollution was more easily broken down.

The current types of mass transportation, such as buses and trains, are also polluters, since they rely on gasoline and diesel engines or electric power. But because they can carry so many more people, they pollute less than if all those people drove their own automobiles. The ideal would be a mass-transportation vehicle which didn't pollute at all.

One of the more recent proposals along these lines is a craft propelled by magnetism. The concept, developed by two scientists at the Massachusetts Institute of Technology, is electromagnetic flight. The vehicle, shaped like a 100-foot-long tubular railroad car, rides about a foot above a concrete guideway. The car would stand on wheels when at rest and in stations. Theoretically capable of reaching speeds of 125 miles an hour, the magnaflight vehicle is levitated by an interaction between coils on its underside and two conducting strips set into the grooved guideway, between which is a winding strip that produces a traveling-wave magnetic field which powers the craft. Such a train, obviously, would not be a source of pollution along its right-of-way. The pollution would be concentrated where it could be controlled: at the electric generating plant which provides power for the circuit.

We are at the dawn of great revolutions in our energy policy. In the future, solar energy, harnessed directly or through winds, tides, and oceanic currents, will generate pollution-free electricity; water will be decomposed by electrolysis in hydrogen and oxygen. Liquid hydrogen will be distributed in much the same way as methane and propane are sold today, and it may power our cars as cleanly as it boosted our space ships to the moon.

No Bugs, No Chemicals

It is possible to control weeds and crop pests without taking recourse to chemical agents. In Florida, a weed control program was put into effect which utilized neither chemical nor mechanical destruction in freshwater lakes that had become overgrown. The agent of control was a Siberian fish, the white amur. Scientists estimated that 100 of these fish, ranging in size from two to 20 pounds, could eat a ton of weeds a day and still not upset the other creatures in the lake. The weeds had become a problem because they clogged irrigation ditches and channels used for drainage. Manatees, the vegetarian sea cow, could also be used to clear the channels from the invading water hyacinth.

There are many natural substances which can be used as herbicides and pesticides, but

*One way of clearing river beds and navigational channels of unwanted vegetation would be to let a plant-eating **manatee** do most of the work.*

the problem is that in large-scale farming—which is as cost conscious as big business—these alternatives are too costly or too laborious to use. But they are ingenious. Males of some insect species have been treated with X rays and made sterile. Introduction of screw worms treated in this way has largely eradicated this pest after a few seasons.

Synthetic hormones have been sprayed on infested areas to cause premature emergence of larvae, which are unable to survive. Bacteria harmful only to specific species has been successfully used. Sonic devices that kill insects that come within range have been used to protect grain. Techniques are being explored to break down natural defenses and render pests vulnerable to predators.

Approaching the problem from the opposite direction, scientists have developed 22 varieties of wheat that are resistant to the Hessian fly. The fly population has been so reduced in California through use of resistant wheat that it is now possible to plant nonresistant wheat again. Resistant strains of other food crops are being developed.

One such strain is a fast-growing cotton plant which reaches maturity earlier in the growing season, before the deadly boll weevil reproduces in large numbers. Cotton farming was a natural place to begin looking for alternatives to chemical pesticides because, of all the major crops in the United States, no other is as besieged by pests. In addition to the boll weevil, which bores into the plants and destroys the young fibers, there are bollworms, budworms, cotton fleahoppers, sider mites, and whiteflies all ready to attack the plants. Consequently, tremendous amounts of pesticides have been used to protect the crops. Though cotton farmers in the U.S. work only 1.5 percent of the cultivated land in the country, they use almost 50 percent of the agricultural pesticides sold in America. The potential for developing the short-season cotton strain—which is smaller than the traditional type but which can be planted more closely in the field and yields the same or more per acre—has been known for many years. But the research was not pressed until the use of DDT was banned.

It would also be wise to consider changing our farming methods from single-crop operations to polyculture. With a more balanced mixture of plants, there would be more ecological stability and a diminished need for the excessive chemical controls we use today, for it often happens that agricultural pests develop an immunity to chemical poisons.

*Contour plowing keeps some soil from being washed away, but **agriculture on a large scale** usually requires the use of massive amounts of pesticides.*

In It Together

Any move toward rescuing the sea from death requires cooperation—among individuals, between industry and government, and among nations. The most logical area for hope is also the area where hope seems to be the most remote: the international arena. It is the only ground where solutions on a global scale theoretically can be found to problems of a worldwide nature.

Sometimes an emergency arises which demands international cooperation. Such was the case in 1971 when an oil spill occurred in the Perisan Gulf. An Iranian company was working on an Italian-owned petroleum rig. The spill affected the waters and threatened the shores of several Arab states bordering the Gulf. The accident immediately became international in scope and demanded the cooperation of several governments in order that a solution be reached.

Outside of such crises, however, the history of international agreement is much less than satisfactory. Negotiations are frustrated by petty differences between nations, or traditional jealousies. Occasionally there are legitimate differences of opinion or conflicting goals. But ultimately, all the diverse goals are one—the maintenance and preservation of life on earth as we know it.

Attempts at achieving accord can often be ridiculed, for they sometimes are reduced to sham and mockery. A 91-nation conference convenes for a couple of months to determine what regulations should be made governing, say, the use of the sea floor. The meeting breaks up two months later with no

*Efforts of groups like the International Whaling Commission are designed to lessen the **threat of extinction** facing many species of whales.*

agreement, and the individual representatives say that they don't know whether enough progress was made to justify calling another meeting, but they always do.

For years, generations, even centuries, it has been an accepted fact that no one owned the ocean, that the seas were free. But all that means today, in an age of offshore oil prospecting and deep-sea mineral mining, is that anyone has the freedom to exploit the oceans. They can overfish, pollute, destroy, and kill without intruding upon anyone's domain.

There are areas of international agreement that have been worked out concerning the sea. The various fishing accords—excluding those dealing with territorial limits and fishing grounds—have generally been successful. And, if nothing else, the International Whaling Commission and various sealing conventions have nations talking to one another. But there has really been no successful or meaningful international conference on protecting the sea from pollution or on controlling or cleaning up pollution. And this is a most serious problem, for the standing "crop" of plastics and oil on the high seas is increasing each year. Plastics are virtually indestructible naturally and even oil has been found to degrade into long-lasting residues. It was once thought that oil slicks, because they disappear after a few weeks, were eliminated naturally, but scientists have found that toxic residues, although invisible, spread out in a wide area affecting marine life harmfully for a period of time up to a couple of years.

But the all-important topic is really well known. The United Nations Conference on the Human Environment at least acknowledged its existence. Now, perhaps, since the problem is defined, we can begin solving it. This is where the hope lies. We must have hope. Or else we will have nothing.

A Fallacious Philosophy

The cause of some of our ecological problems can be found in some of our misconceptions regarding the quality of life we can afford. One of the most deeply entrenched attitudes of western man is that he is superior to and has dominion over nature. Early man lived directly off the land and felt a kinship with it. His respect for earthly processes was reflected in his naming as gods some natural forces and phenomena. His attitudes, and those of some eastern religions today, manifest no competition between man and nature —both are of the same biosphere. All life is part of a complex relationship in which each is dependent upon the others, taking from, giving to, and living with all the rest.

Man put himself at the top of this symbiotic system, providing protection for cultivated plants and domesticated animals and expecting food and other products in return. In our society these relationships have been taken so far from nature they appear almost artificial. It has created the illusion that man has shameless dominion over other life. Finally we have reached the point where we take more useful materials from our environment than we return to it. Our actions are similar to those of a newly evolved, badly adapted parasite that kills its host and thus seals its own doom. Our host is our planet earth, and we must soon realize that it is imperative that we return to it what we take from it, and that we must not be allowed to destroy any other part of the earth's vital system with our wastes. A look at any modern city will convince us that we have a very long way to go to return to unity with nature.

Another attitude we have is that we can ignore with impunity the effects of our activities. We must begin to understand our environment and the natural processes of earth. We must not blithely continue use of

substances in huge industrial quantities without knowing what they will do when they are released as wastes on an unprepared ecosystem. We should understand what has already been destroyed and why it was lost, so that we can guard against further losses. Today a half-million different substances enter the ocean from our civilization. A shortage of vital ecological knowledge keeps us from evaluating the effects of these substances on marine life.

The third and perhaps pivotal attitude that could destroy our world is that we simply don't want to pay our own way. A clean and balanced environment will cost money. We are willing to buy conveniences, but we are unprepared to pay the price it costs to manufacture and dispose of the luxury without harm to the environment. A polluting industry has a competitive advantage over a clean one. This should not be allowed to continue. Those who destroy the environment must

*Liquid by-products from **an oil refinery** contaminate water supplies; fumes affect air quality.*

be penalized for that destruction, even though what has been lost may not be recoverable. The penalties should be severe enough to discourage businessmen from thinking of the fines as merely part of the operating expenses. Unless we eliminate the economic edge of pollutors, the whole world will have to foot the bill.

141

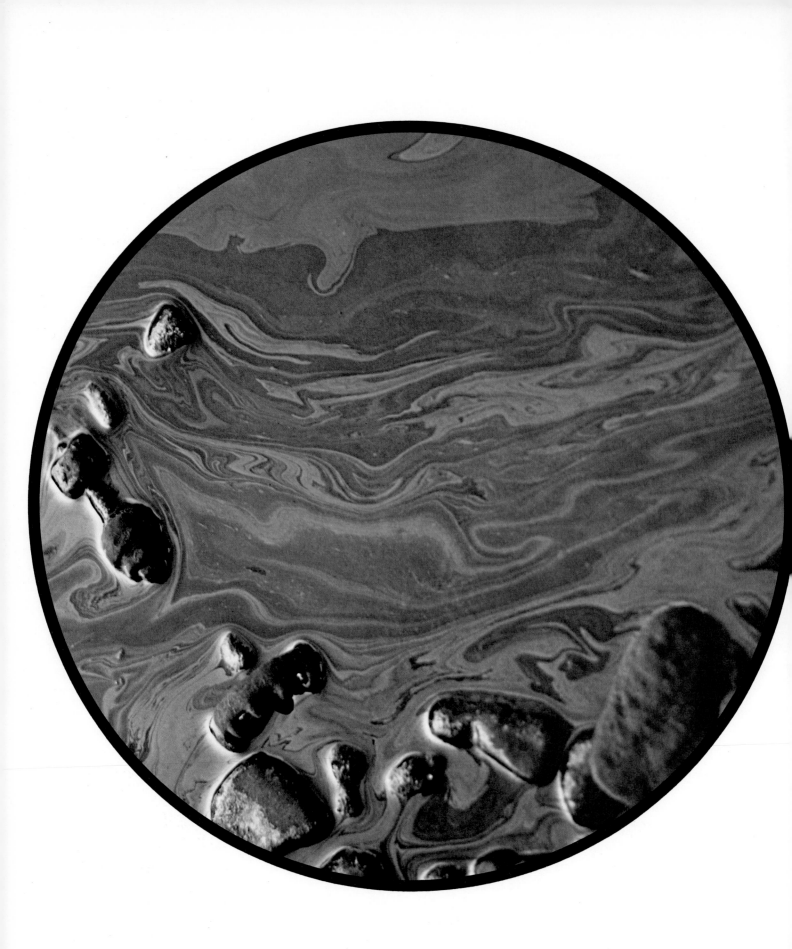

Index

A

Agreements, international, 115, 139
Algae
  brown, 98
  red, 98, 99
  yellow-brown, 98
Amur, white, 136
Anchovy, 42, 49
Anemone, 99
Atmosphere, 64, 66
Atomic power, 102-103
Automobiles, pollution and, 68-69,
  134-35
Azodrin, 101

B

Balance of nature, 96-105
Barnacles, 99
Bioconcentration, 28
Blackfish, 46
Blowfish, 48, 49
Bonito, 44

C

Cadmium, 31, 52
Carbon, 27
Carbon dioxide, 21, 24, 26, 28, 31,
  64, 68, 70-71
Carbon monoxide, 31, 64, 68, 69, 135
Caribou, 104
Carp, 45
Catfish, 45
Champlain, Lake, 116
Chlorine, 39, 53
Cobalt, 20
Cod, 42, 43, 44
  ling, 42
Continental shelf, 12
Convention for the Conservation of
  Fur Seals, 109
Copper, 24
Cormorants, 10, 11
Coto de Doñana (Spain), 38-39
Crabs, 45
  Sargasso, 105
Critical zone, 12-15
Croaker, white, 33

D

DDT, 28-29, 32, 33, 80, 82
Detergents, 57, 89
Dinosaurs, 96
Distilled water, 52
Dredging, harmfulness of, 56-57
Dumontia, 99

E

Earth Resources Technology Satellite
  (ERTS), 116
Ecosystem
  balance within, 96-105
  natural checks in, 100
  Sargassum, 105
Eels, 105
  lamprey, 91
Electromagnetic flight, 135
Emphysema, 69
Energy

  geothermal, 133
  nuclear, 102-103
Environmental Protection Agency,
  58, 129
Erie, Lake, 31, 34, 91
Eskimos, 104-105
Eutrophication, 88-89, 90

F

Factory ships, 40-41
Feather-duster worms, 23
Federal Water Quality Association,
  55
Fimreite, Norvald, 95
Fine activated carbon effluent
  treatment (FACET), 129
Fish flour, 48
Fishing, 36, 46
Fishing rights, 110, 115, 139
Fungicides, 19

G

Galápagos Islands, 115
Geothermal energy, 133
Geysers, 133
Gold, 24
Greenhouse effect, 70, 71

H

Haddock, 42, 43
Hake, 42, 43
Hemocyanin, 24
Hepatitis, 24, 31, 79, 127
Herbicides, 19, 36
Herring, 42
Hessian fly, 137
Hildenbrandia, 98
Hillary, Sir Edmund, 64
Hong Kong, 79
Honshu, 40
Hudson River, 19
Hyacinths, water, 136
Hydrocarbons, 68
Hydrogen sulfide, 34, 89

I

Insecticides, 19, 101
Inter-American Tropical Tuna
  Commission, 115
International Maritime Consultative
  Organization, 112
International Whaling Commission,
  108, 139
Inversions, atmospheric, 66-67, 69
Iron, 20, 24

J

Jacks, 29

K

Kanawha River, 92

L

Land use, 130
Lead, 16, 20, 52

Lobsters, 45

M

Mackerel, 44
Manatees, 136
Manganese, 20
Manta ray, 45
Mariculture, 36, 126-27
Marine protein concentrate, 48-49
Mediterranean Sea, 24
Menhaden, 48
Mercury, 16, 31, 52, 62, 94
Methyl mercury, 16
Milkfish, 127
Minamata disease, 94-95
Minerals, 20, 24
Mussels, blue, 99

N

Nematode worms, 50
New York City, 90, 120-23
Nickel, 20
North Pacific Fur Commission, 109
North Sea, 24
Nuclear power, 102-103

O

Ocean
  buffering action of the, 26
  foreign substances and the, 20-21
  in danger, 116-23
  oxygen and the, 22-23
  threat of destruction of the, 10-23
Oil spills, 56
  international cooperation and, 139
Overfishing, 36, 41, 42, 44
Oxygen, 22-23
Oysters, 126-27
Ozone, 72

P

Pelican, brown, 82
Peregrines, 32-33
Periwinkles, 99
Pesticides, 15, 28-29, 32-33, 39, 80,
  85, 100-19
  cotton and, 137
  natural substances as, 136
Petalonia, 98
Photochemical effect, 68
Piranhas, 91
Pollution
  air, 64-73, 116, 123
    methods of dealing with, 133
  and mass transportation, 135
  automobiles and, 68-69, 134-35
  detection of, 116
  detergents and, 57
  mercury, 94-95
  natural, 62
  need for international cooperation
    in dealing with, 139
  New York City and, 120-23
  noise, 93
  politics and, 106-15, 119
  population explosion and, 74-81
  problem in dealing with, 119
  thermal, 92
  water, 8, 9, 10, 14-15, 16-17, 19,

Pollution, water *(cont'd)*
    20-21, 24, 27, 31, 34-35, 36, 39,
    46, 50, 52, 58, 72, 82, 90
    methods of dealing with, 128-29
Polychaetes, 105
Polychlorinated biphenyls (PCBs),
    39
Polyps, coral, 17
Pompano, 44
Population explosion, 74-81
Porpoises, 41
Protein deficiency, 48
Purse seine, 41

R

Radioactivity, 102-103
Ralfsia, 98
Redfish, 43
Red tide, 36
Reefs, coral, 10, 17, 24
Ribbon worm, 105
Rockfish, 43

S

Salmon, 39
    coho, 91
Salt, 26
Sandworms, 127
Sardines, 42
Sargasso Sea, 105
Sargassum, 105
Sargassumfish, 105
Screw worms, 136
Seahorse, Sargasso, 105
Sealing, 109
Seals, fur, 109
Sea nettle, 92
Sea squirts, 24, 44
Sea urchins, 44, 45, 91

Seawater, electrical and electrolytical
    properties of, 24
Sediments, pollution in, 16
Sewage treatment, 50, 52-53, 54-55,
    126-27, 128
Sharks, 22
Shrimp, 49
    opossum, 92
Smog, 68, 135
Snails, 99
Spearfishing, 46
Spoonbills, 39
Sport fishing, 46
Starfish, 99
Stratosphere, 72
Swordfish, 95
Synergism, 68

T

Tektites, 62
Terns, 39
Thermal pollution, 92
Tide pools, 98-99
Tilapia, 127
Tin, 24
Titanium, 24
Torrey Canyon, 34, 57
Trenches, 12
Trilobites, 96
Tuna
    exploitation of, 42
    fresh, 45
    Japanese fishing industry and,
        40-41
    mercury in, 95

U

United Nations Conference on the
    Human Environment, 139

V

Vanadium, 24
Viruses, 24
Volcanoes, 62, 63

W

Waste, 8, 15, 16-17, 19, 20-21, 24,
    46, 48, 50, 58, 90
    dumping of, 112
    overfishing and, 44
    solid, 60-61, 73
    treatment of, 52-53, 54-55
Water
    cleaning up of, 128-29
    distilled, 52
Weed control, 136
Welland Canal, 90, 91
Wetlands, 84-85
Whales
    blue, 109
    fin, 109
    gray, 109
    humpback, 109
    minke, 108, 109
    right, 109
    sei, 109
    sperm, 109
Whelks, 57, 99
Wolves, 104-105
Woods Hole Oceanographic
    Institution, 126

Z

Zinc, 24
Zooplankton, 28

ILLUSTRATIONS AND CHARTS:

Howard Koslow—66 (top).

PHOTO CREDITS:

Gail Ash—131; Bruce Coleman Inc.: Jen and Des Bartlett—42, J. Brownlie—108-109 (bottom), Bruce Coleman—89, John S. Flannery—35, 117, J. Foott—76-77 (bottom), Neville Fox-Davies—2-3, S. Jonasson, F.L.—63, Leonard Lee Rue III—12-13 (bottom), R. N. Mariscal—79, N. Myers—18, Oxford Scientific Films—90, Joe Van Wormer—39 (bottom), G. Williamson—108 (top); Robert Dill, U.S. Navy Undersea Laboratory—61 (bottom); Freelance Photographers Guild: J. Baker—120-21, FPG—30, 123, Peter Gridley—68, Malak—111, Tom Myers—34, 43 (bottom), Robert Pastner—59, Dick Swift—37, John Zimmerman—137; Jack McKenney—29, 46; Magnum Photos, Inc.: © Bruno Barbey—73 (bottom), W. Eugene Smith—94, 95, Bill Stanton—93; Richard C. Murphy—86 (bottom), 91, 98, 99, 122, 130 (top), 132 (top), 134-35 (bottom); NASA—19, 70-71 (top); Photography Unlimited: Ron Church—11; David Schwimmer—52, 55 (top), 69, 77 (top), 88 (top); The Sea Library: John Bright—134 (top), B. Campoli—112, D. Chamberlain—33 (bottom), Jim and Cathy Church—32-33 (top), 97, 126, Hal Clason—100-101, B. Evans—16, 17, George Green—48, Anne Harrington—38-39 (top), William L. High—44 (bottom), 45, William L. High, National Marine Fisheries Service—43 (top), 114, Tom McHugh—67, 118, 119, Jim Morin—49, Chuck Nicklin—138, G. A. Robilliard—105, Ron Taylor—47, Valerie Taylor—22, Paul Tzimoulis—61 (top), 78; Tom Stack & Associates: Ron Church—25, E. R. Degginger—58, 71 (bottom), 92, Keith Gillet—28, Malcolm F. Gilson—73 (top), Jay Lurie—75, John Madeley—5, Milt Mann—40, Larry C. Moon—72, Tom Myers—26-27, 41, 83, 128, Kenneth R. H. Read—57, Tom Stack—84-85, 103, 104, C. C. Wendle—51; Taurus Photos: Jack Youngblut—53; Time-Life Picture Agency: Kristen Benedktssons—110; United Nations—80-81, 107; Wards, Coral Reef Photographers—102.